A BRIDGE SO NEAR

SHAKIL A I DAWOOD

Shakil Ahmed Ismail Dawood was born in Kenya in 1960 and has lived and schooled in London since he was a child. He went to university in the capital. He discovered his vocation in poetry at a relatively late age, at thirty-three. His life's basic ideal and philosophy is the thought, practice and words of kindness.

**PART OF THE
ASPECTS OF THE HEART SERIES
VOLUME NINE.**

Cover: Architecture, Fountains & Bridges
The Tower Bridge, London, RF Image,
with Many Thanks To Everyone at

KINDLE DIRECT
PUBLISHING

INTRODUCTION

This volume is entitled 'A Bridge So Near', because the bridge we seek as human beings – between our impasses and succour lies in our very humanity. It is this humanity that is the subject matter of this verse. I have tried to show some of the meanings of this:

Every life is a panorama – that much can be guaranteed about every human existence; it is the poet's special task to use this panorama as his stock-in-trade and then delineate his or her life's experiences in intelligible manner.

Thus from the life I have breathed, imbibed and reflected on emerges once again another volume of poetry. Some of this verse was written in 2001, the other more recently.

I am sometimes surprised at what has been allowed to concern me in life; equally I have been surprised at my own concerns and how I have depicted this.

If this volume of poetry stirs the imagination of the reader, and he or she raises an eyebrow at having it positively stimulated, I will have achieved my task in writing this volume. More than that is a boon of life.

I would like to thank my good friend David Udoh for helping me so ably to proof read the text.

A BRIDGE SO NEAR is dedicated to my beloved uncle Osman Mamoe of Capetown, South Africa.

A BRIDGE SO NEAR

▶ ▶ ▶ ◀ ◀ ◀

THE
POEMS

▶ ▶ ▶ ◀ ◀ ◀

MAJESTIC HONOUR

The adult who asks for love
Asks too much

Love is so hallowed,
So great,
The adult does not have the right
To ask for love,
And to even to be loved
Ought to be beyond
his or her expectations

If love is bestowed upon an adult,
It is to be regarded as the greatest elevating,
The finest raising of stature,
And the most majestic honour possible:

Yet you, my little child,
Have the right to the love of everyone
And everything
It is your natural right

How elevated,
Hallowed,
Risen in stature,
Powerful
And great
Must you be, little child,

If the finest,
Most precious
Greatest
And most important
Quality in the universe
Love
Is yours,
As your innate right!

Tuesday, 11/10/2011, 11.23 a.m.

BELIEF

Any thought, word or act of belief
Any kind of belief,
If it does not see and witness
Goodness, kindness and love as imperative,
As the only guidelines to humanity,
Is an aborted belief,
Falling very short of the Truth.

Thus, the religions and philosophies of the
world
Need to reform themselves,
Until their only expression is
Love, goodness and kindness

And when the faiths and philosophies
Practice the sole critical importance
That of goodness, kindness and love
They will represent the Truth
Regardless of the name or title
Of that religion or philosophy.

SUFFICING ACT OF LOVE

There is so much inherent
In your least action,
O beautiful one,

There is so much beauty
In your least deed,
Thought or word,
That if it is bestowed
It will be more than sufficient
To assuage for a lifetimes sorrow.

Thus beloved,
Do not be remote

Even if we
Could not see you,
And were utterly blind,

If you were to once
Glance upon us,
And even if we
Could not perceive
You glancing at us,

This one action of love
Small for you,
Will more than suffice us!

Saturday, 13/04/2001, 9.40 p.m.

FACULTY OF UNDERSTANDING

A flower possesses
The faculty for deep understanding –
Because, it succeeds in alleviating human pain
and sorrow:

The heart
Is the seat of the best understanding,
And the flower hence possesses great heart:

The heart creates the mind,
And the great heart of the flower,
Possessing tremendous understanding,

Confers upon the bloom a brilliant
mind and intellect:

What then of the beauty
of the soul of the flower?

My friend
Possesses fully the faculty of understanding;

Thus she fulfils every criterion by which
A great heart, a brilliant mind and intellect
And beauty
Can be judged and estimated by.

Wednesday, 16/03/2016, 9.35 a.m.

A POEM IN PROSE TO TOUCH AND SPEAK

You have the greatest personality, the little infant, inside you; you look at the world through the beautiful eyes of the little inner child;

You touch, speak and think with the hands, heart and mind of that little child within you: your touching, your words, and your thought are thus true greatness.

Who am I then, not to love you?

Sunday, 28/02/2016, 5.45 p.m.

THE JUDGMENT OF THE OCEAN
A POEM IN PROSE

This life is a river – this world entire is the stream of a river. The collective existence of mankind is a river that inexorably makes its way to the Ocean.

Whatever we do, think or say is washed down-stream, to become One with the Vast Ocean. Our poisons are carried to the Ocean to become diluted – ineffectual and impotent. And our flowers are given the Vast domain of the Ocean to flourish.

Our fragrance is carried, first by the river and then that Ocean's breezes to influence great new expanses. And our apparatus to oppress is smashed by the force of the current at the mouth of the Ocean.

So, beware, that you only accrue good in this life, because then you can be perpetuated by the Ocean.

Only goodness has the strength to undergo the trial of the raging waters. If you achieve evil, the river will give it to the Ocean for Inspection, and because evil is weak, the Ocean has no Option but to smash it out of existence, once and for all.

Evil cannot survive the torrent at the gulf of the river and the Ocean: only the Truth is strong enough to withstand the tremendous Energy of the river's ultimate destiny.

Only goodness thus, can pass the test – to be deemed immortal by the Ocean.

Monday, 26/03/2001, 5.10 p.m.

SIGHTSEEING,
A POEM IN PROSE.

In order to enter heaven, we need to take our own responsibility – we need a full, knowledge of the world.

To see the sights of the world then, one needs to be away from home. The natural home of the chosen is the lap of God.

The most fortunate of us have the natural desire and freedom to roam the world, in our own stead, on our own, and then, the journey complete, one day enter heaven and witness the wonders there.

To become sightseers, it means that the fortunate in their travels have to leave the lap of God, their natural home.

But separation from God is grief: therefore, those who successfully experience the world, in order to explore heaven, are never free of grief – because they have to be apart from God in their travels!

But, "Separation is more union than union." Separation thus exceeds the reward of heaven – and in this life to boot.

How great then is grief, if it exceeds and is more important than the reward of heaven? Grief thus, is a greater experience than the achievement of heaven.

It is the ultimate stage in life's journey.

Thursday, 05/04/2001, 3.53 p.m.

THE BEST TEARS

Weeping ought to be most
valued by our fellow man;

The best tears are inward tears:

For, man does not value tears
Tears that appear on one's face
Are seen as mere rain by man,
And man does not value rainfall
He does not realize that rain falls from heaven,
And that tears are the outpourings
of a greater heaven
The home of God, the human heart.

Man cannot, given his makeup,
Understand tears,
Someone's weeping,

So the best tears are inward tears,
That man cannot see!

Friday, 06/04/2001, 2.30 p.m.

EXCUSES,
A POEM IN PROSE

The moon's only excuse is that she needs energy to grow fully. And after that expenditure of energy, she needs to rest. And, after the good life, she also needs to slim again.

The sun's only excuse is that it daily at dusk, needs to report to God about man's world, which it has been discharged by God to light.

Daily at dusk, after seeing what it has seen on man's earth, it needs heaven's consolation and support: in order to gather enough inner strength, and hope and faith in its mission.

And this is to give man a radiant world – to create the perfect lighted platform and stage and to act out his life's drama.

And my only excuse is that I fret – that the moon and sun don't simultaneously suffuse my world.

Each of these orbs takes a half share in my existence. And I worry that after the daily exit of one of these brilliant cosmic phenomenon, that it might, being tired, retire permanently.

I worry for the wellbeing of the moon and sun. So I am excused if I do not partake of the world – I am occupied with concern for the blazing star and his nocturnal alter ego.

My fear is that they may contract man's contagious disease of indifference – and avail of a restful retirement, in the calmer pastures of the heavens.

Their retirement, however is well earned and their destiny in retiring at last overdue.

Thursday, 05/04/2001, 5.10 p.m.

<u>TEARS OF HAPPINESS.</u>

We weep when grieving,
Copious tears
We weep freely also
When happiness overwhelms us:

They are the same tears
In both instances
Are not grief and happiness
The same things?

Perhaps it is that we weep,
In both instances of sorrow and gladness,
Manifested as undue grief,
Because God has brought Himself
Into our lives –
In intimate relationship with us,
And we are so overwhelmed we weep

We weep due to the grief,
Yes, but mainly
In our joy at the closeness of God:

The tears we shed are
Tears of happiness
Because our souls have truly experienced Him
And we are near His Great Beauty!

Sunday, 08/04/2001, 4.40 p.m.

KNOWLEDGE OF BEAUTY

You possess a good heart:

Your hair is knowledge
As are your eyes

They are full knowledge of beauty

How beautifully knowledgeable
Of the beautiful
Will your words,
Thoughts
And actions be?

Sunday, 28/02/2016, 5.55 p.m.

YOUR QUALIFIED GREATNESS, A PROSE POEM.

You possess a great – the greatest – qualification: the little child has only love to offer: the most beautiful of offerings; and you have love and kindness to offer: the greatest of offerings:

Thus you are the most fit person to talk to a little child, and hold its hand – you are most fit to be thus greatly honoured, which is the finest honouring this world can afford:

Only an honoured, noble and beautiful person can be allowed near a little child: your heart's beauty is your nobility, and your tremendous qualities your honouring and elevation.

Hence you are great enough – qualified enough – great enough, to be the companion of a little child.

Though human beings live by the mind, and most are no exception, it takes the depths of the heart – the greatest human faculty and ability – to appreciate true beauty and nobility – which in truth you possess to an extraordinary degree: for you are qualified to be the companion of a little child!

Thursday, 03/03/2016, 12.45 p.m.

<u>BUYING GOD</u>

I'll yet find my way
Let my remaining qualities stay
In the fight, in the fray!

For, I was lost,
When grief my life crossed,
And, into a void tossed.

Because Love's pain is regular,
And, it is always a road singular,
Patient, I became an exemplar!

Poetry is all I own,
Never to ever be sown,
Growing, without having grown.

Yet, patient, I outshine
Men who haven't paid the fine
For drinking Love's wine!

Though I am now blind,
I am trying to be kind
How will the world me find?

I am to inconspicuously grow,
For I am to tacitly know
God's Face – its ever-present glow!

But now, I can buy God
This at anytime I can afford
Since the road of grief I trod!

Sunday, 25/03/2001, 7.16 p.m.

THE MEANING OF ART

Even if science is fully known,
Reality remains unknown.
That is, until we feel the poetry,
The poetic discourse of Art:

Art gives life to that given death;
Scope to the microscopic,
Dignity to the shamed,
Infinity to the finite;
Thus it arouses the hearts of mankind –
The essence of mankind,
Magnified,
Strengthened,
And cherished
By Art.

Man, unable,
Is made by Art;
Man, discoloured,
Is coloured by Art;
Man, invisible,
Is made visible by Art.

Man, made prostrate by civilization,
Stands tall with Art,
His hand, disabled by industrialism,
Grasps life when absorbing Art;
Made to wear a frown by the world,
He smiles with Art.
Made skeletal by meaningless worldly
existence,
He is given form and scope by Art.

Politicians want man deaf, dumb and blind:
He is given music, eloquence and vision by
Art.

Inexhaustibly,
Art has sung throughout history
The song of man!

Art is light cast to ascertain reality,
Yet unknown,
Or unacknowledged
By man.

Sunday, 25/03/2001, 10.45 p.m.

FAITHFUL TRUST

The sea is faithful to its remit
To solicit man's welfare
In visiting wave after wave
To his lands.

The moon is faithful to its trust
To allow the universe to retain some light
That is, hope,
In its darkness.

And the sun's attribute is its fidelity
It lights up the day
So men can clearly
See the beauty
Of their fellow men and women.

And you, personally,
Have more responsibility than all this
Your heart contains every sublime quality

Which, if you access,
Will be faithful to your trust:

To make amenable
The successful transaction of lives,
Bring succour and scope to the hopeless,
And make humanity available to itself:

In short,
You possess every ability
To enable and achieve the flowering
Of your life,
And the blossoming
Of the lives of others!

Tuesday, 10/04/2001, 12.34 p.m.

GRIEF AND GOD

I had to abandon life,
A life I loved.

I had to consume the banquet
Of Crafted, Bestowed grief,
And then, sink deep
Into the ocean of trouble,
And brave its storms,
Without any seafaring means.

He
God
Especially ordained
All this pain for me

He, the Beautiful One,
The Remote,
Proud,
Separated One,
However, had considered me

In all this
Especially considered me
For His Attention

His least Thought of me,
And the Devotion of some of His
Precious Time for me,

His Regarding of me
I think is the height of honour
For, whenever He Pays Attention
To someone in this manner
He means to honour the heavens
And the cosmos;

That He, Who could Unconsciously
Allow the universe to operate –
Its people left alone
To fully practice their free will,
Has Consciously decided
to embrace someone

With His Personal Consideration.
Pain and grief therefore
Are the height of the greatest honour

And privilege
Possible in the universe,
For they are Considered

Bestowal by Him.
And I am thus
Especially honoured and privileged.

At the very least,
In any case,
I was in the Conscious Mind
Of the Most Important One:

At the very least,
God, the Great,
Remembered me!

Wednesday, 11/04/2001, 4.37 p.m.

THE INVESTOR

You are going to be very wealthy one day
Because of your tremendous investments:

You have heavily invested
The beautiful qualities
Of your heart –
Goodness,
Kindness
And love
Everywhere
You have sowed them
In the hearts
Of animals and people
In this universe,
In the heart of the universe,
Which lies in the hearts of people
And animals

Your investment will grow
It has to grow
And magnify
For the lovely nature of it

Comes complete,
with innate nurturing,
Looking after
And guarding
Attributes that are built
into the very nature
Of majestic investments like yours

If the universe itself grows,
It will grow well

Thus your investment of the virtues
Is the essence of the universe's growth,
And hence the universe
is made for people like you
Its very heart,
The source of its growth,
Is commanded by people like you.

And rich and richer you are to become
If this is your basic wealth,
How wealthy will you become
When your great investment
Matures over time?

Sunday, 28/02/2016, 9.47 p.m.

YOUR EDUCATION

'Education leads to wisdom; the educated person, accordingly, is the wise one.' Imam Ali ibn Abu Talib.

May your education be
empowering, replete:
May by it you become greater,
more complete:

May your learning be such,
others may from it benefit,
To be fully given action and
speech by knowledge's permit;

May, when you put pen to paper,
profound is the result,
That to ignorance and other human
blight is the perfect insult;

It requires a thinking heart and
mind to complete an individual:
May you be completed so: hence,
wise, compassionate, successful!

Education leads to kindness:
kind, loving, good conduct,
May of the finest education
you be a truly great product!

And on par with your great virtue,
may you be awarded,
With happiness, greatness and
success spiritually rewarded!

My dear, I wish you true realization
of every great possibility,
To you I wish a beautiful heart and mind:
the finest quality!

Go your way into the world,
armed with your great education,
And you are the pride of humanity,
and each community and nation!

Thursday, 31/03/2016, 7.15 p.m.

CONSIDERATION

To un-create consideration
Is the hardest task,
For consideration is born in the heart
The home of the Divine:
The Divine,
Which is indestructible

Consideration
Is the powerful weaponry of the heart
Which cannot be denied
So powerful is it,
It can bring to ruin
The strongest citadel
Of indifference and uncaring,
And so constructive is it,
It can bring a shambles
Into a blossoming garden,
With immortal blooms

Consideration
Hence is the mightiest force
In the human universe

There is none mightier,
Because consideration is Love!

Thursday, 31/03/2016, 7.55 p.m.

A POEM FOR A CONSIDERATE WOMAN, MAN OR CHILD.

Today I was forlorn,
Negated
By an indifferent world
I almost ventured into slavery
To pessimism

But then, I thought of the potential
Of persons like you:

A heart that is to become truly great;
That comes with innate courage;
A heart that is dying to everything negative,
And becoming alive to everything great

Love, goodness and kindness
Are the assault weapons
Of this heart,
That batter down the negative

With strength and versatility;
Caring is the sun of your attributes,
Which sheds light for the universe,
And sweet is your implacable attitude
To impart affection

Your concern solely for a forlorn victim,
To give her or him a massive, violent overdose
Of love.

Yes, today I felt oppressed
But your potential,
And your being ever-ready to implement
Your heart's greatness
Emboldened me,
And made me look far beyond

Into the beautiful future I transcended
And smoothly travelled,

Whilst an inhabitant of the here and now
That future suffused me,
Whilst I was in this world
That competently, copiously donates
indifference

And its malevolence
Became a nothingness to me

Your heart took me far
As far as heaven
Because my pain disappeared
Only the heavenly can do this

Who says heaven
Is not built
By the considerate heart,
A heart like yours?

Thursday, 31/03/2016, 8.45 p.m.

I VOWED TO LOVE YOU

I vowed to love you
Always,
Forever

And you
Were the grateful recipient
Of my great, faithful love
And loving loyalty

I vowed
To love you
Always,
Forever,
Until the end of time
And I did so

And when the end of time arrived,
For the first time
In our relationship,
You came near me:
For the first time
You actually held my hand:

For the first time,
You deigned to talk to me:
For the first time
Since I fell hopelessly

In love with you,
You let me look
Into your lovely eyes:
And then you said,
Emphatically:
"Feast your eyes
"You are allowed now,
"To feast your eyes
"To their satisfaction
"To surfeit
"Upon my Beauty!"

THE VALUE OF IGNORANCE!

The stars know nothing,
Know nothing,
Save to bestow their wealth
Of jewel like brilliance
In the dark sky
The stars are unknowing

The moon knows naught,
Knows naught,
Save to grace with its luminosity
A gravely opaque world
They – the stars and moon
Are unconscious,
Unaware

Would that man
Was as ignorant
As the stars and moon

And would only know,
And show
One of his qualities

His great capacity
To donate,
Without fee,

Without any expected return
The brilliant light
Of his great love
To his fellow man,
Whose world is now so
Overwhelmed by darkness!

Saturday, 14/04/2001, 9.52 p.m.

RELIGION

Love,
Goodness,
And kindness
Are religion in its entirety:

True religion is a light cast
In our darkness
Our darkness
Of indifference and hate.

The light of religion
Is its luminosity of goodness.
This is the largest sun ever in existence,
A life-giving sun,
Dispelling the sleep upon us.

Yet this sun's beams
only inspire kindness,
The real truth

So simple
Yet so profound in implication.

But religion reserves its final message,
Its entire content,
Its greatest reward
The ability to love,

To those who accept and practice its
truth
Kindness!

Monday, 16/04/2001, 5.17 p.m.

FINDING GOD

I had psyched myself
Never again,
Never again
Will I be charmed
By a beloved,
To be ensnared
In the tentacles,
The vice-like grip of Love.

One glance at You, however,
And my carefully constructed armour fell

Voluntarily,
One conversation with You,
And I relinquished
My vows
I reneged
An ardent effort
Of years

For You are a Beloved
One in a billion
Nay, trillion
Nay One Wholly Unique
And I happened to chance upon You.

There was no chance anyway,
That I may have avoided You
Avoided Your Great Trap
Your Magnificent Beauty

I had to compromise
My most deeply set wish to be free
To be free of the pain of Love

Alas, I am now so free,
I am alone in my Love,
Lonely, bereft of You.
The pain will have to be worthwhile!

Monday, 22/04/2001, 11.25 p.m.

YOUR BLOSSOMING

The sunlight shone
On your face,
Especially for you,
And the waters of the ocean
Came landwards,
Towards you

And the ground of my heart
Became foundation
For your love

And you blossomed
Into a flower!

DO NOT BE DESPONDENT!

If you are down,
Burrowed in depression,
Remember,
You have fallen because
You are beautiful
And handsome
You are heavy
With true and real life!

So then,
If despondent,
You love,
And care,
You do it with
More weight,
More gravity,
And more importance
Than when you are
Light with happiness!

Wednesday, 25/04/2001, 4.35 p.m.

MESSAGE

Loving,
You are
Love itself

Lovingly,
You love,
And,
Love tells me
That you are
Lovely with
Loveliness.

Thursday, 26/04/2001, 1.30 p.m.

TRYING: LOVING IS TRULY TRYING

Trying is truly trying,
For one can only gain ground
In order to laugh
By first weeping;

Loving is truly trying
For, to authentically
Manoeuvre to
The site of love
One first has to lose
All mobility!

Trying is truly trying,
For to direct sincere effort
In order to realize love
We need to kindle light
From the fire of our souls;

Loving is truly trying,
For to lovingly
Attune to a beloved,

We first need to experience
Our own shattered hearts,
That we may know the rules
Of decorum
Of love and loving.

Friday, 27/04/2001, 9.47 p.m.

GRACIOUS INTENTIONS

In the tribulation of life,
You shall be well equipped:

Clothed in grace,
Immersed in inner strength,
Surrounded by an aura of dignity.

I hope you will be steadfast,
For your way will be
That of great ones in dilemma

The citadel,
The apex of humanity's mountain
Beckons you:

Your intentions virtuous,
Your creed kindness,
Your emblem love,
Your vision truth,
Your vocation faith,
Your gaze direct:

In this storm of a life,
You are well equipped to swim
Against the inevitable tides.

I wish you well.

Friday 14/05/2001, 11.15 a.m.

WITNESSING THE BELOVED

Forever,
Always,
We want to have vision
Of you;

For, to witness you
Was the sole purpose
Of our sight

But,
A mere single glimpse,
A single fleeting glimpse
The simple hint
Of a glimpse
Of your face
Is enough
It is surpassingly fulfilling

For,
It opens up our vision
Both inward and outward,
Wholly,
With total encompass,
To all things!

Thursday, 17/05/2001, 7.32 p.m.

MESSAGE FOR MY BELOVED

My beloved,
I will do everything for you:

My wealth,
My knowledge,
My love,
My faith
Everything
Whatever I have,
I will share it with you:

I will not even shed
My full quota of tears
For myself;
I will reserve portion
Of my fund of tears
For you,
As yours,
To be shed on your behalf.

Tuesday, 22/05/2001, 10.55 p.m.

SUNSET AND THE TIDE

You may be forlorn
You may be crestfallen,
But nature is the ultimate healer

To watch the sunset
Whilst sitting on the rocks,
Is to watch the world begin its rest,
A comforting sojourn in to night-time,
And to emerge resplendent and new at dusk

To welcome the sunset,
The sky is bedecked in wonderful colour
Inviting the moon to take a rightful place
In the heaven's kind activities

The whole sky
Then becomes dynamic
With beautiful forces
The stars that love to spend their energy
shimmering,
The buoyant moon,
That loves to float unsupported,
And the sun,

Like a great potent potential of nature
Hidden in the bosom of all this kindness
And love
The kindness and love of nature

Love then, is the keynote of nature
In all its beauty,
And the sun loves to set,
Perhaps just for you,
Sitting on the rocks

For it – the sun
Lives to make humanity happy,
And brings warmth to all
To all individually
To all as unique individuals

You are the special individual
The sun has chosen to set for today,
And the waves bring news to you
Of nature's immortality!

WOMAN WHO SMILED AT ME.

You used
Much, much less
Than an atom's worth
Of the entire love
In your ample heart
And gave it to me
By smiling at me

And I am ecstatic,
Filled to surfeit with love

But, I am not selfish

I wonder,
With the greatest admiration,
At how much love there is
In your capacious heart,
How much capacity
For conferring joy

Upon your fellow men, women and
children
You possess

And love
Is the most beautiful action
That can be conferred

By a beautiful human being
Given your scope for beautiful action
then,
How beautiful are you?

And loving
Is the height of wisdom in action
How wise are you then
In reality?

Love
Was designed
As the best
The greatest
Quality:

You were designed
As the best
And greatest
Human being

Because,
You love!

SHE SMILED AT ME

Thank you
For telling me,
So articulately,
So volubly,
So voluminously,
About love

But we've never met before,
And will probably never meet again
Nor did we speak when we did meet

You merely smiled at me!

MOST LOVELY

Kindness
Is the most beautiful
Attire
And inner world
To possess

Because you are kind,
You are beautiful
Outwardly,
And inwardly!

THE DIVINE

Codified
In your spirit
Is that ultimate greatness
Love

Thus,
Codified
In your spirit
Is the Greatest Itself
The Divine!

PERFECT

71

Good intention
Is the perfectly
Working theory

Because,
It is as perfect
As its practice!

<u>BLESSINGS</u>

Blessings be upon you,
Because you are kind

Kindness
Is so great,
It cannot be adequately
Requited

Thus, blessings,
Which fall upon the kind person
Are the greatest entity
In the entire universe,
For they adequately requite
Kindness!

<u>THAT DENIED</u>

You ought to forbid yourself
Everything
Except,
Goodness,
Kindness
And love

In doing so,
You've allowed yourself
Everything!

<u>LOVE'S SEAL</u>

Friendship is the vehicle
That is best equipped
To make deeper
The deepest
Inroads
Into the realm of love –

Thus,
Love's seal
Isn't love,
But friendship!

BE CAUTIOUS

Be cautious
With your love,
Goodness
And kindness

To practice
Love, goodness and kindness
To excess
Is being cautious
With them!

LOVE LETTER: A POEM IN PROSE

You are so far away, out of reach. The only way I can communicate with you is by letter. I want to tell of my love for you, yet how can my hand express at a distance what only my heart can in close proximity?

The ink dries, but the love in my heart grows.

How can you, from so far away, see in my eyes my soul singing? Or weeping?

The Truth I have derived from this experience is this – love cannot be described – only felt!

Words written at a distance seem raw nourishment compared to the ripe sustenance of words spoken face to face: these are anchors for the heart.

I can write expressions of love, but if you were still here, I could look into your eyes and be more articulate with my speech. I can really only praise you when I am cherishing your hand in mine.

Still, my letter will reach you, and with it, a cursory token of my love. But wait – but wait!

We are only separated physically: our love is a spiritual one, one guided by our spirits: spiritually thus we are inseparable: are we not together in our love?

Saturday, 28/04/2001, 5.45 p.m.

AUTOBIOGRAPHY

I was,
I am:
I will be;

I am there,
I am here:
I will stay;

I am tuned,
I am music:
I will sing;

I am charged,
I am light,
I am electricity:
I will shine;

I am quiet,
I am speech:
I will eloquence;

I am bereft,
I am tried,
I am tired,

I am new:
I will try;

I am resigned,
I am endurance,
I am steadfast:
I will envision;

I am startled,
I am late,
I am early:
I will arrive;

I am slow,
I am fast,
I am moving:
I will walk;

I am tough,
I am soft,
I am weak,
I am strong:
I will live;

I am calm,
I am distraught,
I am equal:
I will survive;

I am young,
I am old,
I am alive:
I will know;

I am clever,
I am simple,
I am natural:
I will intelligence;

I am running,
I am breathless,
I am fatigued:
I will rest;

I am soul,
I am heart,
I am brave:
I will succour;

I am just,
I am unjust,
I am justice:
I will ameliorate;

I am willpower,
I am weakness,
I am lost:
I will unravel;

I am student,
I am novice,
I am learning:
I will pray;

I am here,
I am nowhere,
I am somewhere,
I will weep,
I will will,
I will love!

Saturday, 05/04/2001, 5.05 p.m.

CALLING HER BLUFF

I loved you so much
A great, loyal love
That was unrequited

Decades passed by,
And you did not change
Your attitude
And inclination towards me

I was desperate
For an atom's worth
Of your love

And you were absolutely,
Utterly niggardly

In desperation,
I cried out to you:
"Love me,
"Or leave me!"
The latter part of my appeal
I uttered half-heartedly,
To call your bluff

And you replied,
Promptly,
With full conviction,
Full intent
And total self-belief:
"I won't love you,
"But, I will leave you."

The latter part of your reply
You uttered
With absolute certitude,
A certainty
Hitherto not come into being,
And never witnessed
In the world.

MY PROTECTION

What happened,
That the roof time provides
Became absent?

I did not realize,
I had reached the zenith,
And now would be alone
Left behind,
Shelter-less,
Weeping,
Hiding my sorrow
With my weeping
For, this is the land of life
The land of love!

For what is life,
But yearning
A clamour,
A yearning for release?

For what is life,
But to see the world
The burning,

Blazing,
Incandescent world
Through sorrow clouded
Sorrow shaded eyes
Thus protected?

My darkened field of vision
And witnessing
Is my encompassing comfort
And safeguard
Against the world's
Brilliant pain!

Thursday, 17/05/2001, 10.47 p.m.

THE DEATH

She, with intent,
Avidly scrutinized my face
For motive
Ulterior motive
She was most intent
On this intent
And wasn't swayed from it

Her mind,
But most of all
Her heart spoke
Eloquently

Cancelled within her,
Entirely,
Was the expectation
Of goodness

In a brief glance,
Of a few seconds,

She told me
Most articulately
With great clarity
That she expected nothing
From her fellow men and women

In those few seconds,
She painted the vivid picture
Depicting men and women
As selfish,
Untrustworthy,
And iniquitous
What was my relation
To this woman?

I had stopped walking
In the narrow corridor of the supermarket
To politely let her pass by
Most of all,

To show courtesy and politeness
To my fellow human being
And she looked at my face
For ulterior motive

The very few seconds
It took for this lesson to transpire
Told me well:
Men, today,
Have arrived at a state
Where they have lost their faith
And lost their trust in humanity.

Saturday, 19/05/2001, 7.45 p.m.

NATURE'S UNPREJUDICED LOVE!

The waves greet,
And meet everyone,
And take men's faults
Out to the depths!

The rain falls,
And, feels,
For everyone,
And, cleanses their be-soiling!

The breeze hearkens,
And, envelopes
Everyone,
And dries their tears!

The birds welcome,
And, sing
For everyone,
And, heal
Their hearts and souls!

The sun smiles upon,
And, is generous

To everyone,
And with warmth,
Dispels our misgivings!

The moon is a torch
And, beauty
For everyone,
And brings hope
Of the light within man!

Would that man,
Created greater than nature,
Could learn from nature,
And bring love
To everyone!

Saturday, 19/05/2001, 10.25 p.m.

A QUESTION TO MY BELOVED.

I fully know,
To the slake,
That you withhold
Your love from me

Yet all I want
Is for you
To accept my love

Most of all,
I would like to love you,
But this is something
You do not care for

But, your greatness
Cannot – can never
Be taken away from you

So great are you,
So near perfection,
You see none
As unattractive
All, however marred,

Are attractive to you;
All are tremendous to you

And you accept any good deed
From anyone
As the thirsty earth
Welcomes rainfall

There is no reason then,
For you to reject my love

So why do you?

CREATIVITY

When you are near me,
Your glance
Pours into me
What your mind,
Heart
And soul
Have reasoned;

Your touch restores
Realistic feeling
To my touch;

Your speech
Conveys
Moods
And a mental makeup
Carved with rationale
And logic

In other words,
You make me feel beautiful,
For your mind,
Heart and soul

Have reasoned
With love as premise;
And the only realistic touch
Is kind
And real rationale and logic
Can only make all moods
And sensibilities
Appropriate and pleasant:

Beauty,
In other words,
Is creative,
And whenever received sincerely,
Creates the beautiful!

SOLUTION

O you!
Beautiful one!
Glance
Just once
My way,
With a look
Of love

I have witnessed
You life-long
Stare at me
With a frown
Your bad moods
And rage
Not instigated by me

Yet, at the same time,
I know
With utter conviction
That you love me
Deeply and truly so

I know, as well,
That you

Only have good intentions
Towards me:

Is it because you
Have chosen loneliness,
Being alone,
As a life-style,
And that because you love me
So much,
That I would have to be
A partner to you,
If you showed and manifested
Your love for me
That you are indifferent
Nay, feign indifference
Towards me?

Your bad moods,
And rage
Is thus with your own inadequacy,
And not me,
Because you love me
With all your heart!

DEVOTED TO GOODNESS

I looked at the sky
And saw the yearning soul
Of the moon,
Manifested
By its great, precious
And active radiance;

I looked at the night sky
And I saw the stars
With their great intention
To succeed,
However far they may be
From earth,
To give out jewel-like light
To the world;

In all this,
I was in garden
Amidst the great
The blossoms
Issuing generously
Their glorious fragrance
And majestic colour,
And their ample hearts

So evident
And I assimilated
All this knowledge
Into my very bones:
And then, I understood
Your choice in life,
Your attitude to life,
And your chosen path
Of development

I understood your soul,
Your noble inclination to all,
Despite being near some creatures,
And far away from others

And I understood your heart
In other words,
Amidst this garden,
Surrounded by the moon,
The stars
And flowers,
I understood
Your beauty!

A CHILD.

They are talking behind your back –
Positively gossiping about you –

The angels only
Only
And endless
Topic of conversation
Is your loveliness,
Beauty
And perfection!

MY ENCHAINED DESTINY

I have voluntarily
Made myself hostage
To your kindness,
Goodness
And love –

And I know
That I do not desire
Any freedom
From my fate,
And do not wish
Anyone
To pay the ransom
To free me –

In fact, God Himself
Doesn't take any – any – pity
On me,
And will never
Ransom me
From my enchained destiny:
Do they not say,
"He is Cruel,
"yet Merciful?"

THE TRUTH

It was the desire of the Truth
To create creation
For one purpose
Love

And, commensurate
With this Truth
Was that this love
Was most suitable
To be given
Of all beings
To a little child!

THE MOTHER

To witness
A brilliant child
Bedraggled
In every direction of life
Is the special woman's fate
The grieving mother

Yet, she finds the strength
Somehow
From within
To smile at her child
And family

And her greatest power,
Which can never fade,
Or be diluted
Under any circumstances,
Is her love

Her love can never die
Her love is immortal

If there is anything
On earth
That deserves the adage
Of immortality
It is the grieving mother's love
And the grieving mother.

THE BEAUTY OF SORROW

The event of sorrow
Does not miss a beat,
And is always opportune –

But, a deep experience
Of sorrow
Deepens the heart,
Intellect
And soul
Of the one afflicted

And if he or she
Is responsible, to boot,
And kind,
They arrive –
Arrive at the nearest phenomenon
To human majesty

Such is the premium
Of experiencing sorrow
Which then becomes
The most beautiful experience
That can ever be experienced,
And represents
The fullest,
Most complete life lived.

HUMAN KINDNESS

Human beings
Are beyond angels
Made greater –
Angels merely represent God
As ambassadors

Human kindness
Is the Mind,
Heart
And Soul
Of God
Manifested!

A WISH......for Renzie, sixteen year old

I hope you are free of troubles
But into trouble you will stumble:

Then, I wish you strength and steadfastness,
That you may be to real beauty a witness

For authentic beauty is naught but sorrow
The beautiful did this path truly follow

Of their tale may much for you ring true
May your turn come soon – and not be in lieu

May you learn your lesson and really attain,
And thus truth – love and kindness maintain

And may your own tale rise one day very high
Into the hearts of men – beyond heaven
and sky

Why did I come here – and why have
I you found?
To know that your life is with

great destiny bound
What if, on your path, there is no repose?
Then sorrow's made you great,
you may suppose!

THE MEANING OF TEARS

Heaven was made
For tears
The tears shed
By little children,
Good parents
And kind people
And animals

Heaven was built
With their tears,
And for their tears,
And who-so-ever enters heaven
Does so at their express behest!

LIFE

In this two-day long affair
Life
What have I gained,
And where have I foundered?

I gained
Every time I found it opportune
To think, speak and act with kindness;

And I lost whenever I forsook
This opportunity.

But in the final analysis,
I gained in the end,
Because a single instance of goodness
Or kindness
Is so powerful,
It far, far, outweighs
Any lost opportunities
To conduct myself well.

LITTLE CHILD

Your personality
Is that which Prophets
And saints
Emulate

Little child,
You are the Truth
The Truth,
Manifested

You bring with you
To this world
Your Love,
The strong
Nature of a Love which
Was powerful enough
To create creation:

Such is your power,
And Beauty,
The most dangerous action
In the world and universe
Is to un-necessarily interfere
With you.

KINDNESS

With kindness, to humanity an arm stretch
And the magnificent and great will you fetch:

Hence in kindness, you ought to revel,
And thus un-truth's endeavours repel

Kindness is truth, and thus great brilliance,
And of discord and amity, at once, consilience

I am by my experience to kindness bound,
Sometimes, where sorrow is,
kindness is found

For sorrow bound me, fast, to her wheel,
And implacably, strongly I resolved, like steel

By alchemy to make of my sorrow beauty,
Kindness was the conduit and I was at liberty

Kindness, of everything,
has strength and power,
It is garden for life's jails and prison's
their mower:

Where there is kindness, there is the great:
So easy to think of, practice, speak and instate!

A TRUE LOVE

A true love
Is someone
You can trust
Absolutely

You are so responsible,
And with it, loving and kind,
And so good hearted,
You can be fully trusted
By anyone on earth

Thus,
You are a true love
To the whole world!

WITH GOOD CHARACTER

It is said,
'Good character
'sets the good person
'apart.'

How is it then,
That you are not detached,
But attached to so many?

It is said,
'Good character
'makes you
'a feeling
'human being.'

How is it then,
That you are so senseless,
You see goodness in all,
The bad,
And the good?

It is said,
'Good character
'is a characteristic
'of uniqueness
'and individuality.'

How is it then,
That you have merged,
In the sea of the humane,
And humanity,
Until you have lost yourself?

It is said that,
'Good character
'makes one without desire.'

How is it then,
That you ardently desire
Greatness for all,
Everyone on earth?

And it is said that,
'The devoted pursuit
'of good character

'good character alone –
'makes one poor in wealth.'

How is it then,
That in your ample heart
There exist and live
The heavens and the earth,
All the seas and all the lands,
The prayers of all the angels,
And the hearts
Of good parents,
Little children
And animals?

THE OASIS

How precious and valuable
Is an oasis?

How welcome is it
To the traveller
In a harsh and inhospitable desert?

How much can an oasis
Save a forlorn life
A life abandoned to
Extreme wilderness?

You are all these things
In this world,
Now a harsh desert of a world:

How?
Through your kindness!

YOUR EXPRESSION OF BEAUTY

You hold power over me
You are beautiful

You are kind
Caring and
Loving

And this power
You hold over me
Is a welcome restraint to me,
For all it means is that
I love you:

According to the wise,
The best way ahead is with beauty

You way is less than beauty

For you remove
One component
Of that beauty
From the beauty

You remove love,
To be expressly bestowed
In every instance,
And then fully express
What remains of that beauty.

LEARNING DIFFICULTIES

To have learning difficulties
Cannot reduce the acuity of your intellect
For what you most desire in life,
Despite having learning difficulties
Is peace and prosperity.

For every person on earth,
And you can show
Goodness, kindness and love
These desires
For parity and justice,
And the portrayal of great virtue
Are the finest aspects
Of the most brilliant intellect:

However, possessing
This great heart and mind –
Both combined make up the intellect
Is not enough to gain you a university seat,
A thoughtful partner
Who can converse meaningfully,
Nor a constructive role
A responsible one
In society,
One that you so ardently desire!

Sunday, 17 / 04 / 2016, 4.35 p.m.

THE ANGER OF GOD? THE LOVE OF GOD?

The earth's seen my tread
And I saw the earth in dread:

All for falling with Him in Love
Wasn't my Love for God enough?

Does Loving then fall short
Of His Needs Him really distort?

In Loving Him was He so un-glad
That in return He makes us so sad?

Is Loving Him treating Him badly,
That the world is driven so madly?

To Him we stretched a Loving arm,
And all He did in return was to harm:

Both Great Love and God are mystery
This, in Loving Him we didn't foresee

But I know, I know He's Merciful,
Making sad ones most successful

Success, though we are forlorn
For, for success we were born

Pain then is extraordinary success,
That is God's Love in Great Excess
For God could never be hurtful
Hurt from Him – so, so Beautiful?

We are to be great – show patience
Our greatness spirit and sustenance:

Pain hence takes you to heaven's Portal:
Through *pain and Greatness* you're immortal!

Sunday, 17/04/2016, 4.56 p.m.

A MESSAGE FOR YOU.

'The greatness of a man or woman does not depend on their beauty or their handsomeness ; it does not depend on their wealth or their education ; it depends on their heart : if their heart is great, then they are great.' (Muhammad Ali)

The human being is the most privileged creature in the universe. Everything special – and the greatest of stations were designed for the human being.

A human being – any human is a very special individual, being created especial. What is the special character reserved for men, women and children? Goodness – the goodness of a great heart.

The universe is too small to contain God, but the good human heart is large enough to contain Him. The human heart thus can contain all the heavens and the earths, all the seas and all the lands.

But, the human heart needs to be qualified to possess within it the universe – it needs to be good, kind and loving.

Your heart, is loving, kind and good: what power do you then lack? If the loving human heart can contain the stars and the sun, it has within it the power of those blazing cosmic bodies.

Your heart then is as powerful as the stars and the sun. And this is because of your love, goodness and kindness. Every virtuous word, thought or deed increases your great power.

This is the meaning of human greatness, and within you there is tremendous greatness: this is your explicit birth-right, and what you were born for, since you are a human being.

<u>And finally, a piece of prose for my younger readers:</u>

A MESSAGE FOR A YOUNG FRIEND

I hope that life, as you venture into it, treats you well – and if not, that you bear up to life's difficulties with dignity, steadfastness, and fortitude;

I hope that you make patience the anchor of your life and living – automatically, by being patient, you will create in yourself courage; may you have the courage to be yourself, to live for your-self, and not to please others; may you generate thus, by living for yourself, a generous spirit, that is generous to others and yourself;

I hope you develop a balanced and equable approach to life, that will give you insight into human existence and a knowledge of its problems – by inner balance and equanimity you will become a referee in the tribulations of mankind;

I hope the world enrols you and your great talents fully to improve it as a home for flora and fauna – and mankind;

I hope you possess the magic – the alchemy – of a smile and good moods;

I hope your kindness gives you, in return, the strength and power it merits in the kind person, in order that you are least hamstrung by emotional and psychological problems; and recognizing that all need affection,

I hope you develop your power to be good and kind to everyone – the deserving and the undeserving;

I hope your ample heart magnifies as you course into the future, and that by this, you become a great individual; I hope to all poor, oppressed, the disabled, the forlorn an depressed you stretch a kind arm, manifesting your greatness;

I hope your greatness wins you, in turn, the love of another great person:

May you live by love, for love and in love!

Love and best wishes,

Shakil A I Dawood, Thursday, 14/04/2016, 12.57 p.m.

A NOTE TO YOU

This is a note to you, a person who is the doer of good: there is nothing in the affairs of humankind greater than doing good. Hence the moment you do, say or think something good, you rise to the highest state humanity can afford and attain to.

You are a sovereign greater than any earthly monarch. The person who thinks, speaks or acts upon goodness sets himself or herself up for the real throne on earth – the topmost height possible to a human being.

You thus, by doing any good add a golden core and majesty to your being; gold perishes not, and nor does the golden human being.

The moment you are good, you pay the burden of your dues; if sick, to act upon goodness is the source of, and channel to, better health and sanity; it is the focal point of human and Divine wisdom.

No doubt, you, the good person will suffer, but your suffering is a regime by which you become fitter and more adaptable to our difficult world;

Your vantage point and intelligence are increased and unparalleled. Just by adopting goodness, you increase your intelligence.

Your goodness is the love in your mind, heart and soul: *it is not any love*: you have cast aside mind, heart and soul to do good – in other words, what sacrifice could be greater?

Goodness is equally at home in church, mosque, temple, palace and humble dwelling; it is not only the gateway to sainthood, *but it is the saintly.*

The constant practice of goodness makes you steadfast on your way in life, and your way in life cannot then be questioned. Your life is fool-proof in goodness.

Absorb yourself in the Unity goodness brings you to, for you become One with the universe when you are good. And if you weep, if you weep through goodness, you magnify yourself to even beyond all the above.

Then you can bear a thousand sorrows of yours with greater ease, and you will be more easily philosophical about grief. At this point, your apprehension of Truth is unparalleled, and you become that Truth. A drop in the Ocean of that Truth is that Ocean, is it not?

Let your epitaph be, *"There went a good person."* There is no higher, greater accolade. Goodness is the greatest of human qualities and treasures in the universe!

Love and best wishes to you, dear reader.

THANK YOU
© SHAKIL A I DAWOOD
London May 2016

YMm

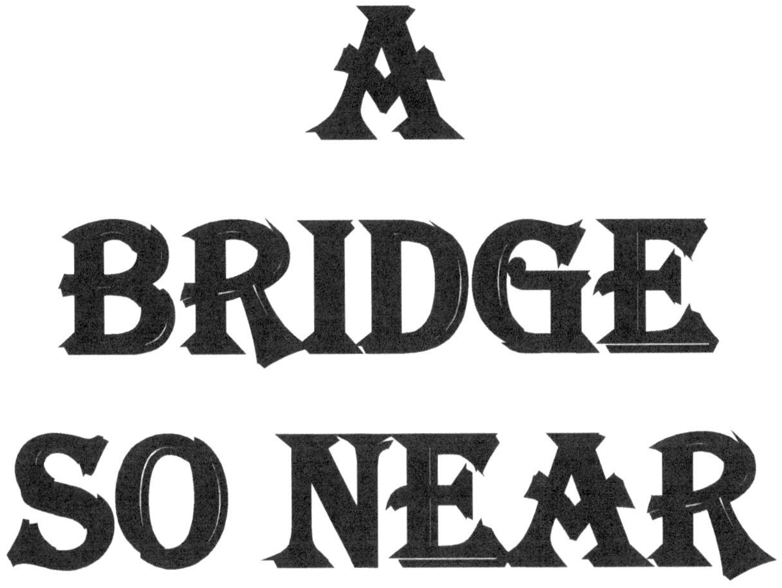

COPYRIGHT
© SHAKIL A I DAWOOD
LONDON MAY 2016

KINDLE DIRECT PUBLISHING

786

FURTHER BOOKS BY SHAKIL A I DAWOOD

THE 500 COMPLETE TWO LINE POEMS

A SPEAR OF GRASS POETRY

IN CONTEMPLATION SELECTED POETRY

GRIEF AND GOD

THE HAIRDRESSERS SALON

A SPIRITUAL ANTIDOTE TO DEPRESSION

KALAM THE PEN

OBSERVATIONS A LIFE EXPERIENCED

IMMERSIONS POEMS

THE VERSE GARLANDS

GOODNESS KINDNESS AND LOVE

ASPECTS OF THE HEART VOL 1

ASPECTS OF THE HEART VOL 2

KINDLE DIRECT PUBLISHING